FLUENCY

Fluency

a collection of asemic writing

Karla Van Vliet

Shanti Arts Publishing
Brunswick, Maine

Fluency
a collection of asemic writing

Copyright © 2021 Karla Van Vliet

All Rights Reserved
No part of this book may be used or reproduced in any manner whatsoever without written permission from the publisher except in the case of brief quotations embodied in critical articles and reviews.

Published by Shanti Arts Publishing
Interior and cover design by Shanti Arts Designs

Shanti Arts LLC | 193 Hillside Road
Brunswick, Maine 04011 | shantiarts.com

Printed in the United States of America

ISBN: 978-1-951651-47-3 (softcover)

Library of Congress Control Number: 2020952780

I've come to the river. I am in that space of feeling before words come, before I can craft some gesture of mark into literary or artistic meaning. The river has long been a place of sanctuary for me. This, the New Haven River, this bend in the river at Sycamore Park. When the summer sun shines, I come to lay my body down alongside the moving water that has run off the Green Mountains. The river is the first line of poem, of song, of gesture toward meaning without the need for meaning, or syntax or even thought. The river is and I am grateful.

I think about this in a new way as I contemplate how to write about asemic writing, a developing art movement that depicts writing-like markings within artworks. At first, I am heady about the subject, how it inhabits an essential space of expression, depicting what is yet fully denotational. But the very thing that draws me to asemic writing is the place it rises from. For me it embraces the mystery between silence—what is yet to be spoken—and the semantics of known language. What is represented are the feelings or ideas that the word, or markings, suggests to the artist and to the viewer.

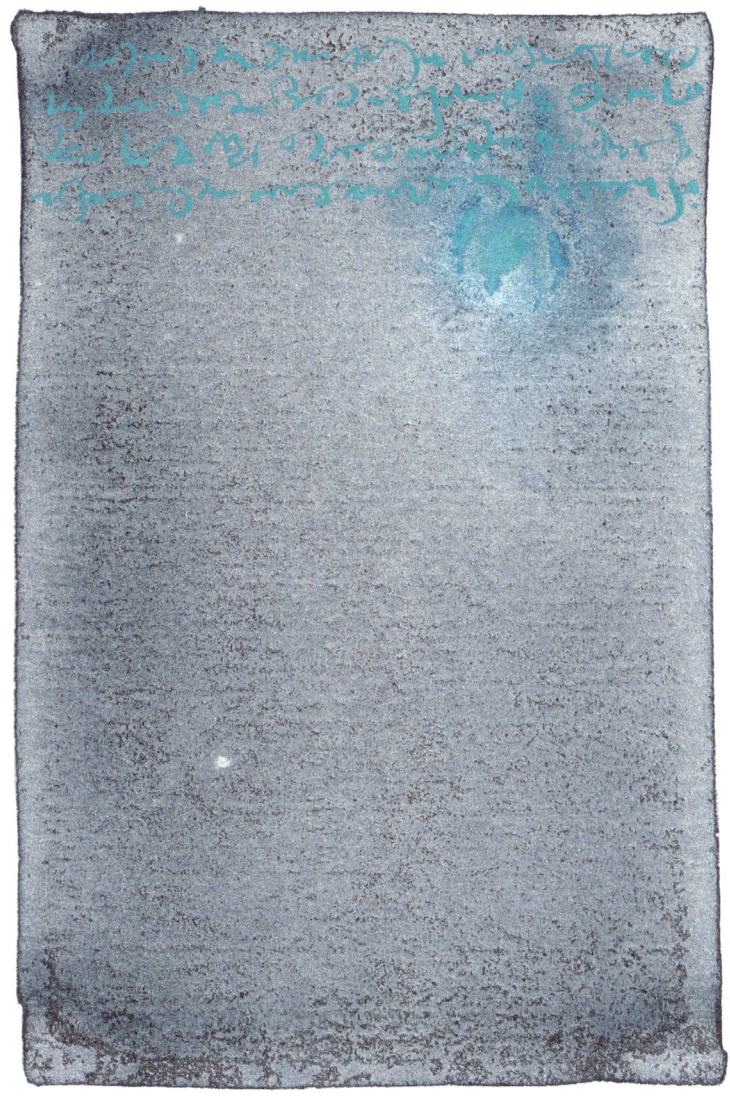

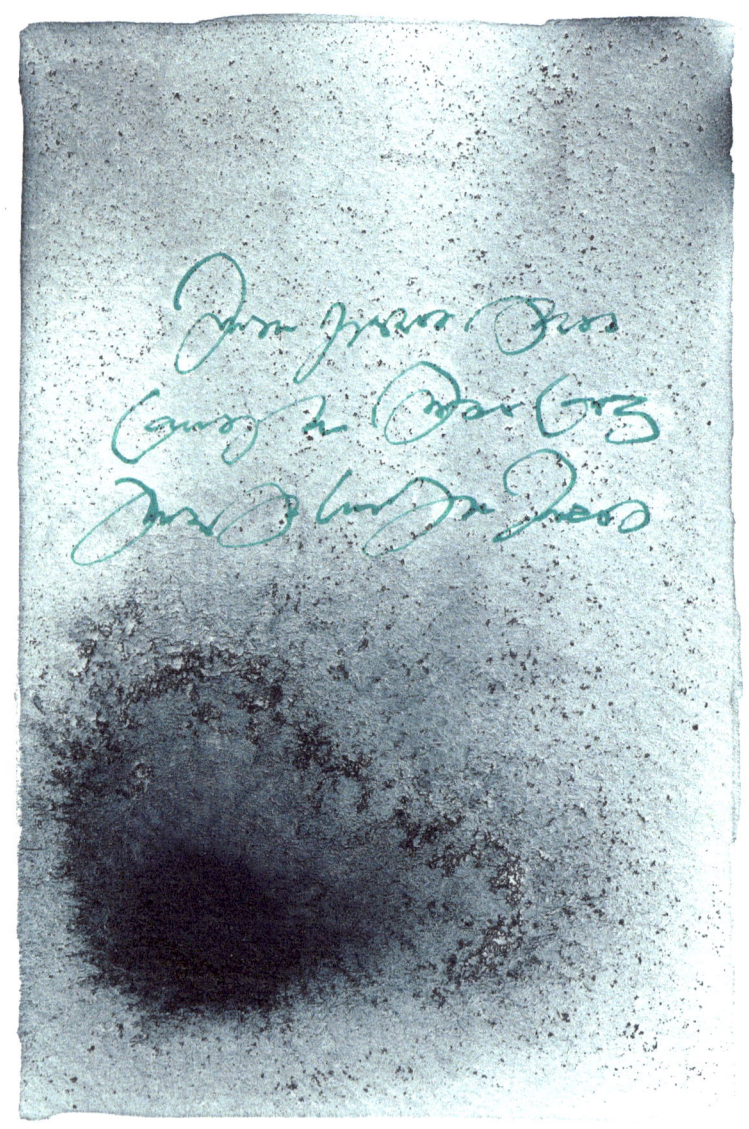

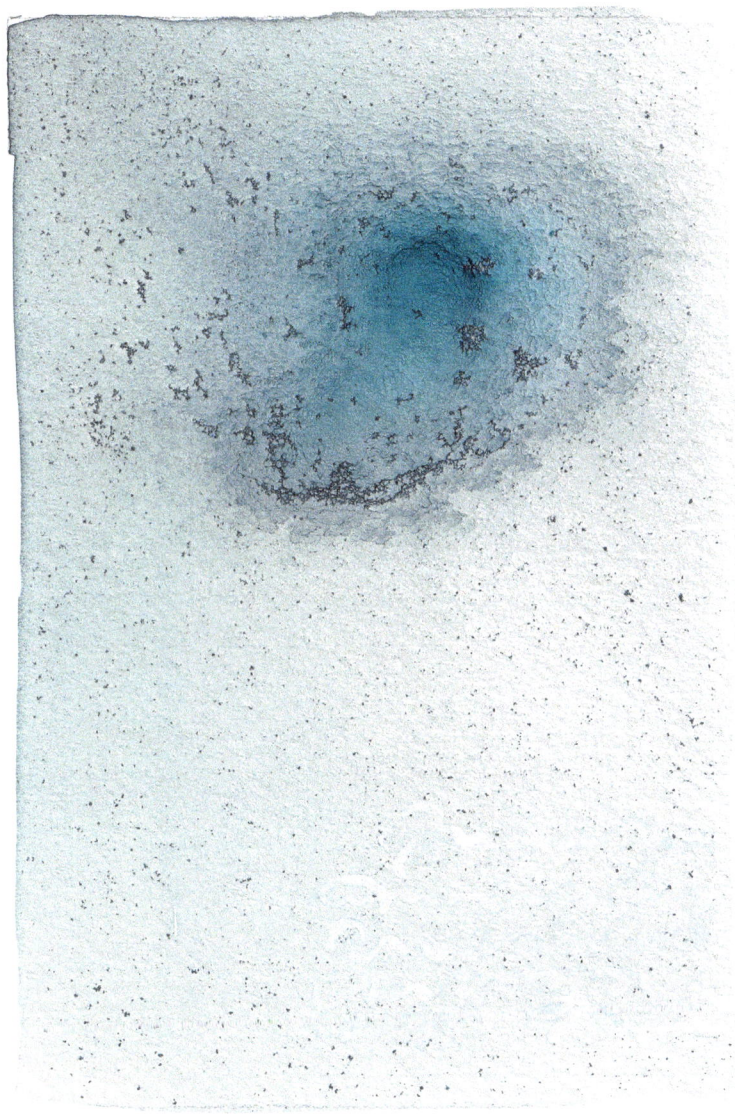

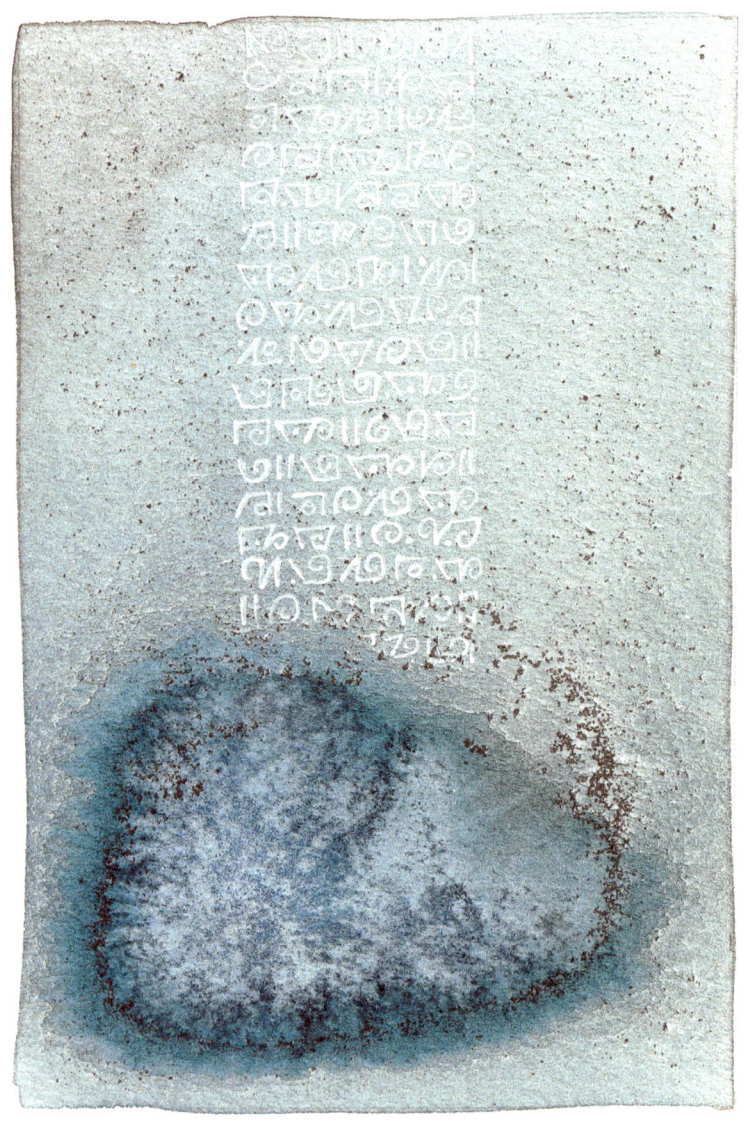

And so, when I undress my brain, toss aside the shirt and shorts of my thoughts, I arrive at the river. Ready to lay down along the dazzling line, the bend, the sharp corner of the oxbow. I let the sun work on me, heat my skin to burn and roll into the cold water that carries the song I long to interpret, which brings me, with its stinging cold, into the experience of my body. The quick inhale. The river is a place of meditation, that deep going into the place of being, and I long for this place which informs me.

It is a place before creation, the place of tuning into what is within me that wishes to be expressed. I am a person who needs expression to stay sane. That's a dramatic statement but I have come to believe that this is the state of an artist, the particular fountain that artists drink from, the need and definition of an artist. At the very least it seems to be what my life has been about, been driven by. I look deeply in and I follow what rises to be expressed letting it come, as it requests, onto the page or canvas. I am an artist and also a poet. What is expressed is set down by mark and line. I am also a dreamwork analyst which has taught me to be a deep listener to the unconscious and what desires to be understood or brought into consciousness, with dreams often being the messenger of that knowledge. Also, an understanding that this knowledge has its own unfolding when we are open to its flow and path. It has been my way to let this unfolding happen, when it comes to expression, on the page or canvas.

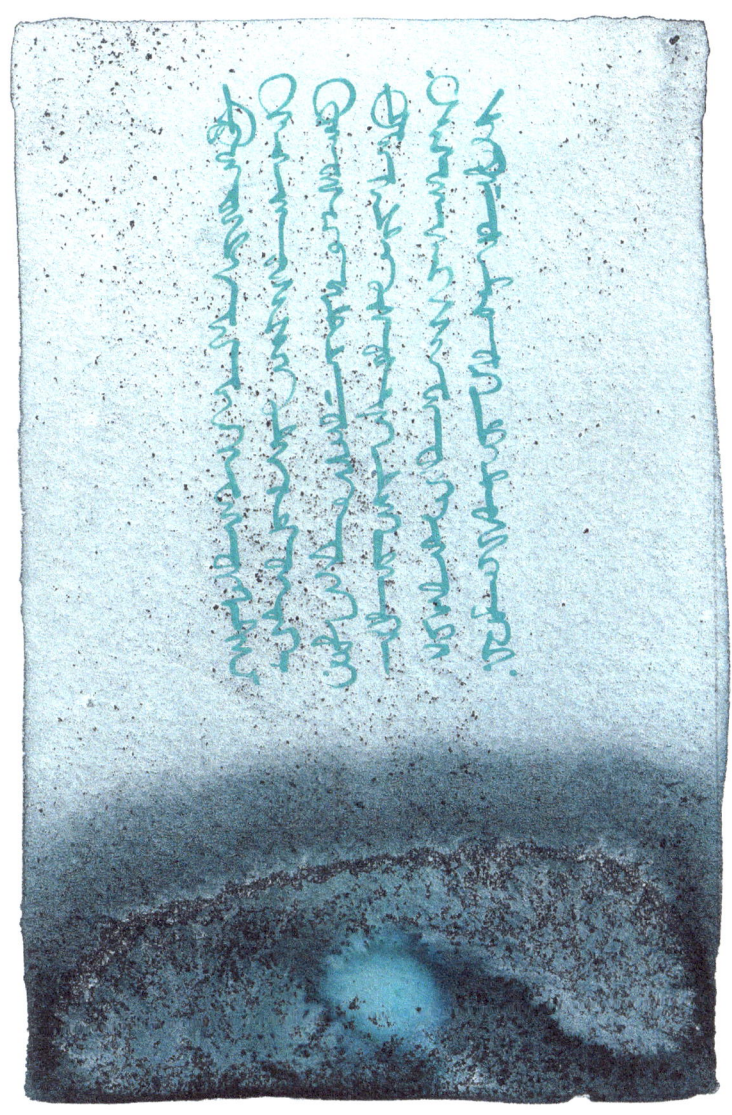

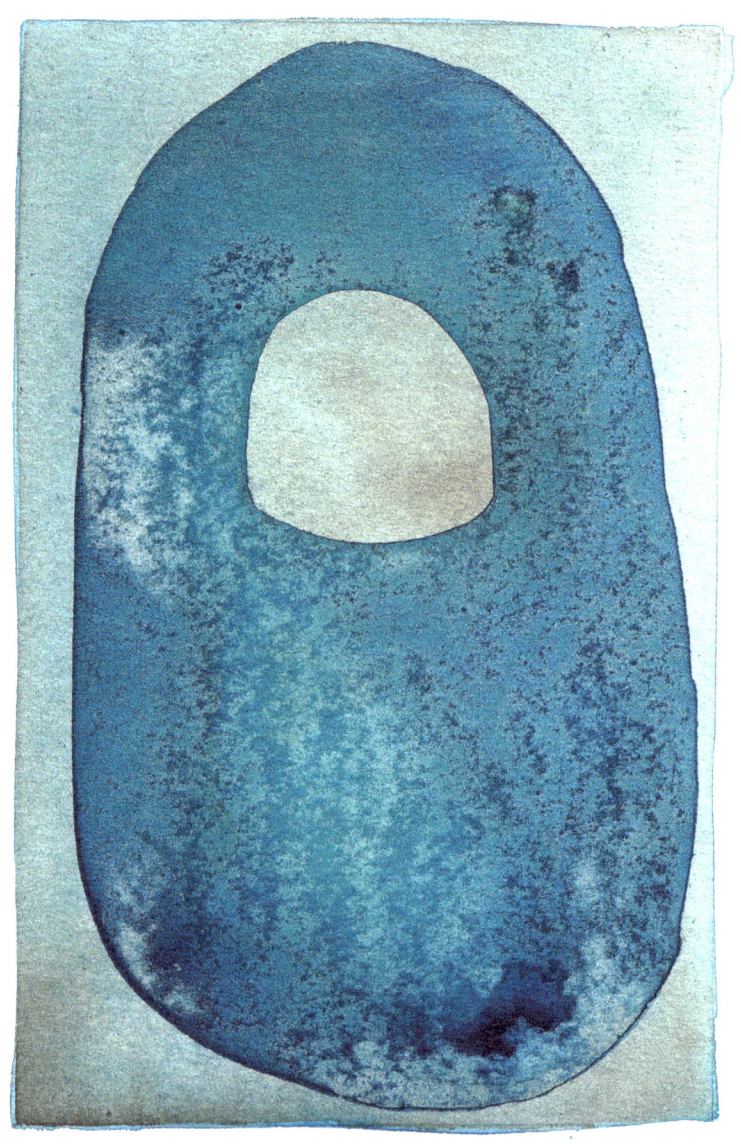

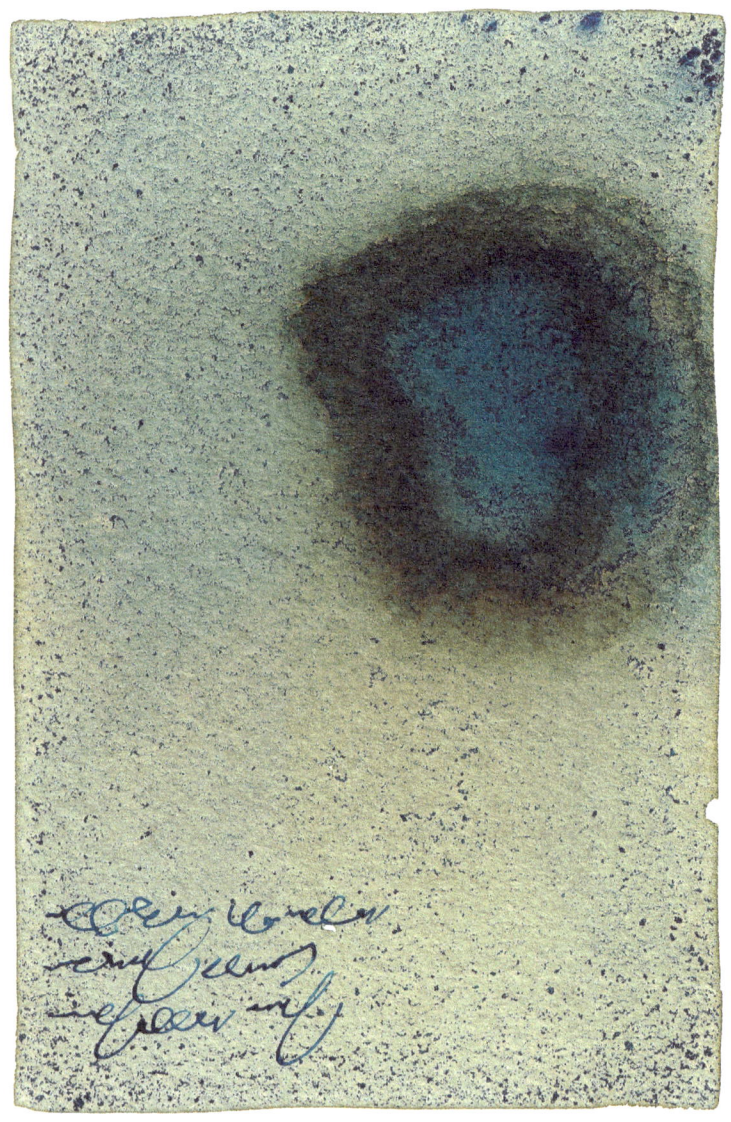

The river is the first line, but there are many lines and marks in this landscape. I close my eyes now and bring myself to the river's edge. It is winter at the time of this writing, and the snow and cold keep me inside. But in my imagination, I can visit and notice the wealth of patterns: the sun arrays reflecting on the water, the tree's branching into blue sky, the heron's footprints in the wet sand, the pebbled bank, the diving sweep of the kingfisher's flight, the jungle of Japanese knotweed, scattered driftwood. These are all marks I can draw from, in some sense they are the alphabet of this landscape I love so, which lives in me and is often the language I utilize to describe my inner landscape in poetry.

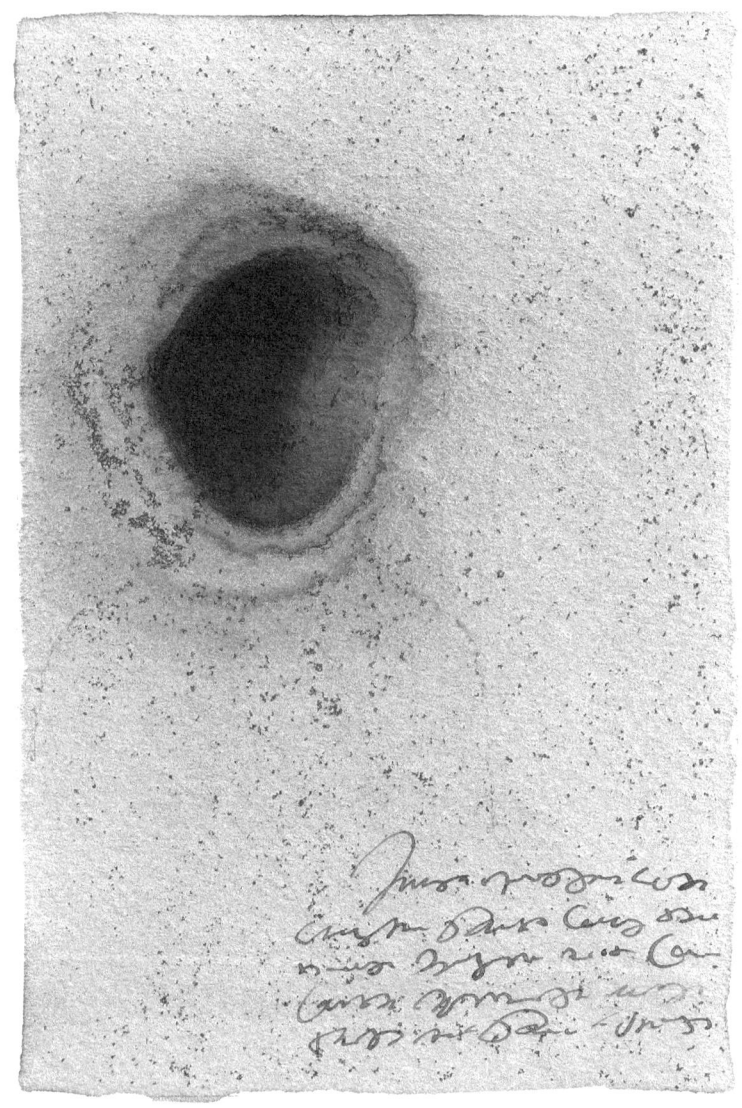

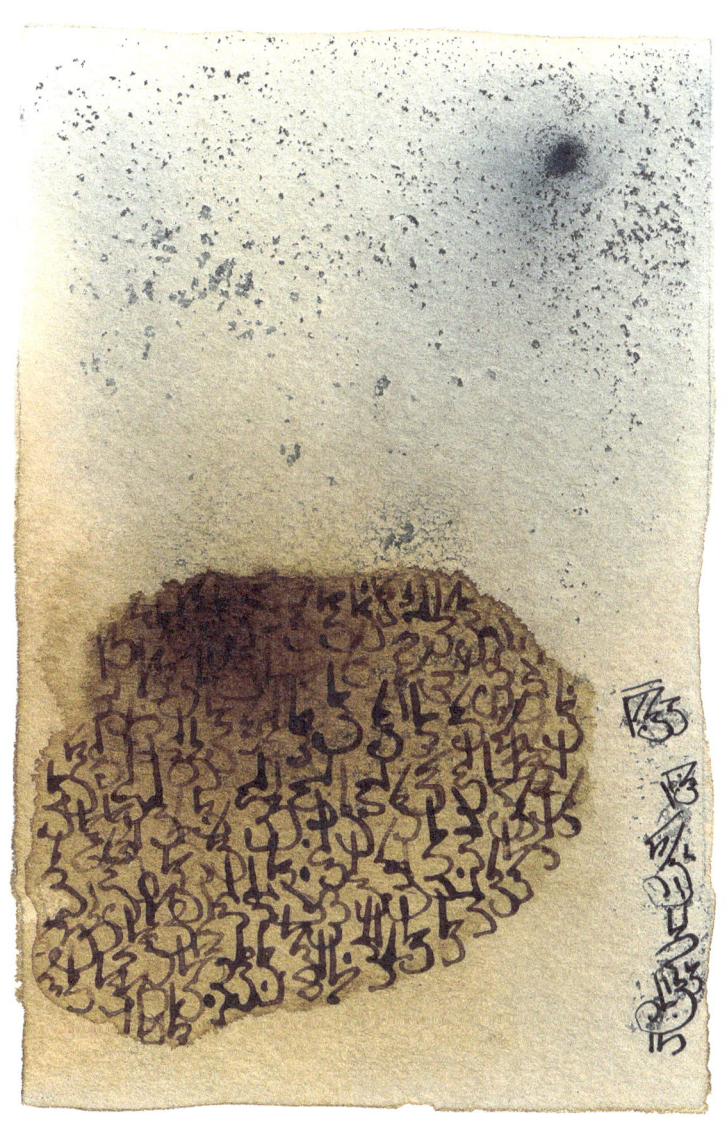

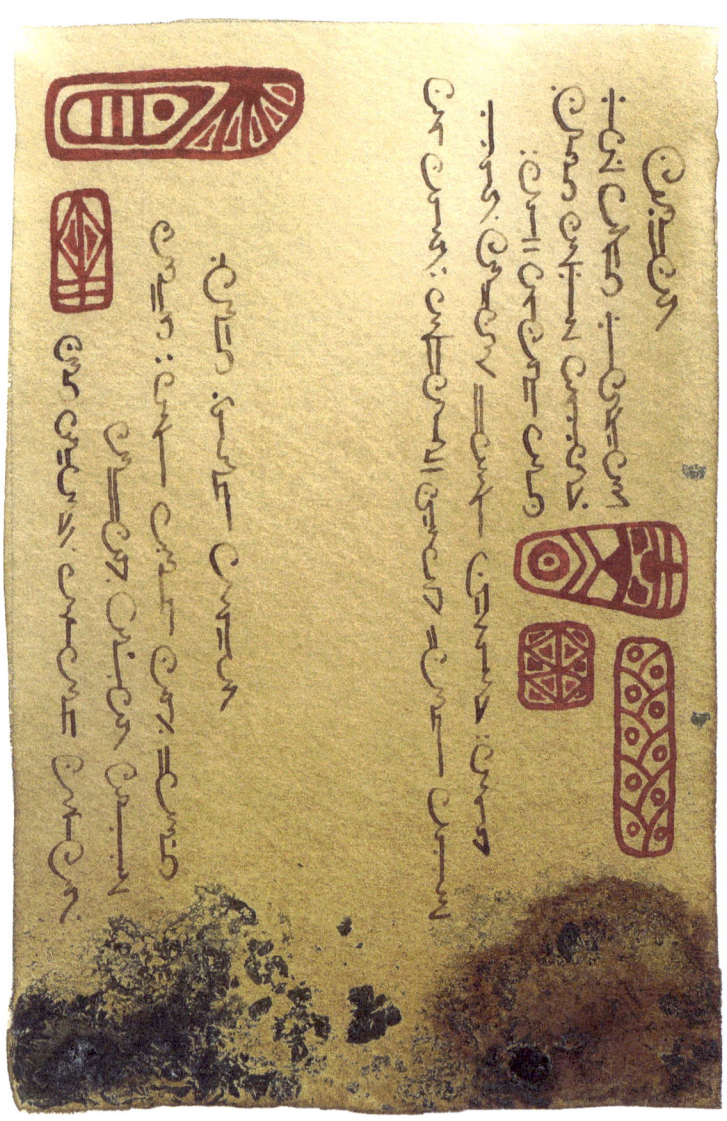

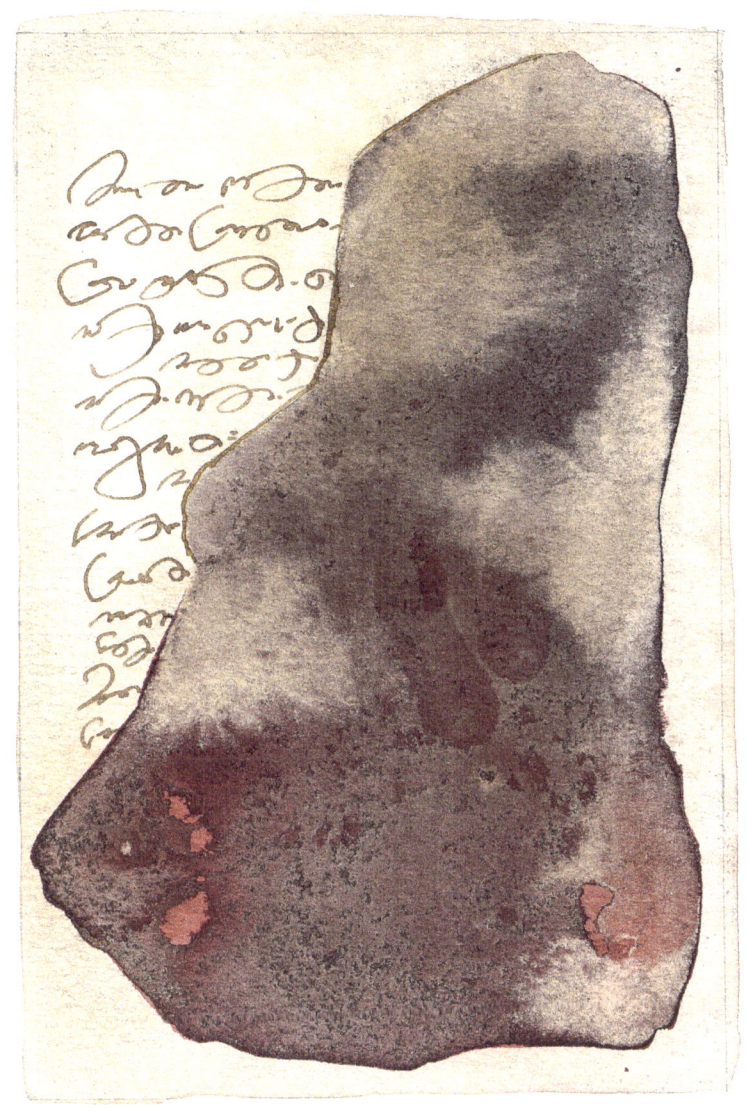

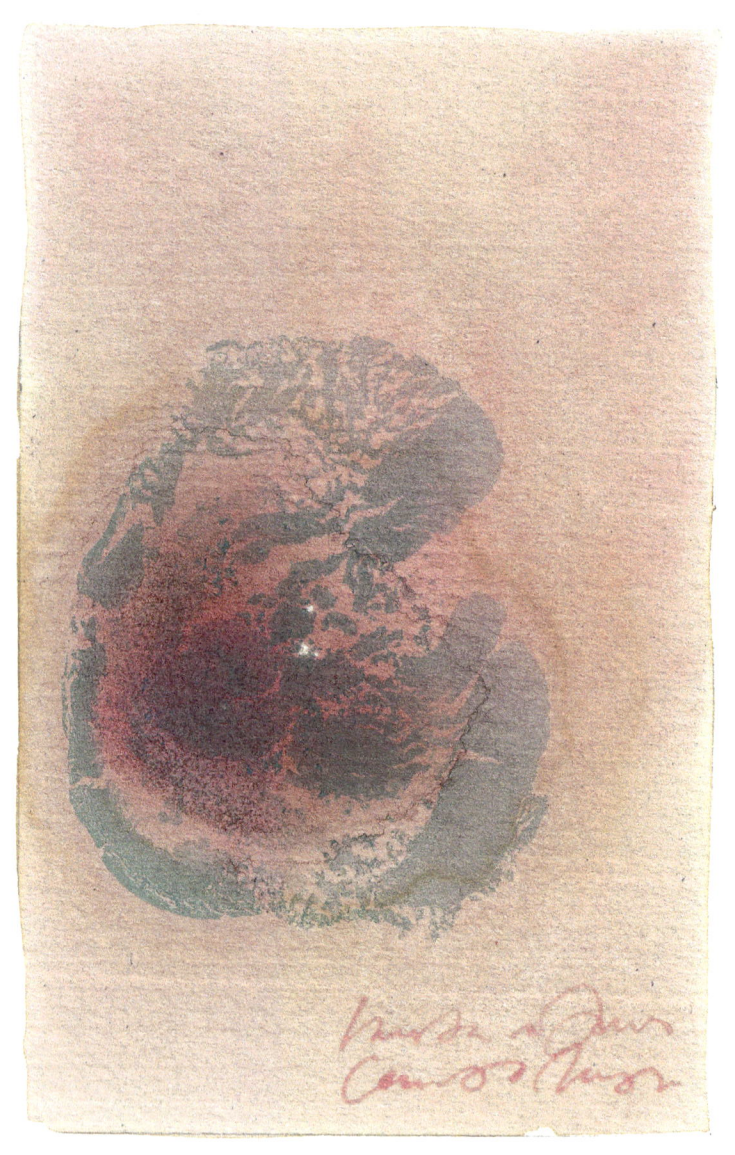

But there are times when I do not have words. Yet I have the need and desire to write. It is to asemic writing that I turn in these moments. To the gesture of writing. Here I find the mark carries the feeling state that cannot be or cannot yet be put into poem. It keeps me in practice. The practice of paying attention to what is often the uncomfortable state of allowing the feelings within to be experienced. Our culture doesn't generally support this with so many ways of distracting ourselves at the tip of our fingers. And yet we die of it everyday, for without experiencing who we are and how we are in relationship to the world we walk around separate from ourselves. What is the point of being alive when we are dead to the experience of being alive? And so I come to the river, on a cold, snowy day or in the heat of summer, metaphorically or literally. I come to the state of being that the river holds for me. A kind of silence and stillness that is full of sound, the water rushing by, the bird's calls, the sound of children playing at times, far off traffic, trees rubbing their branches, and always the hum of insects. All this like the busy mind set aside.

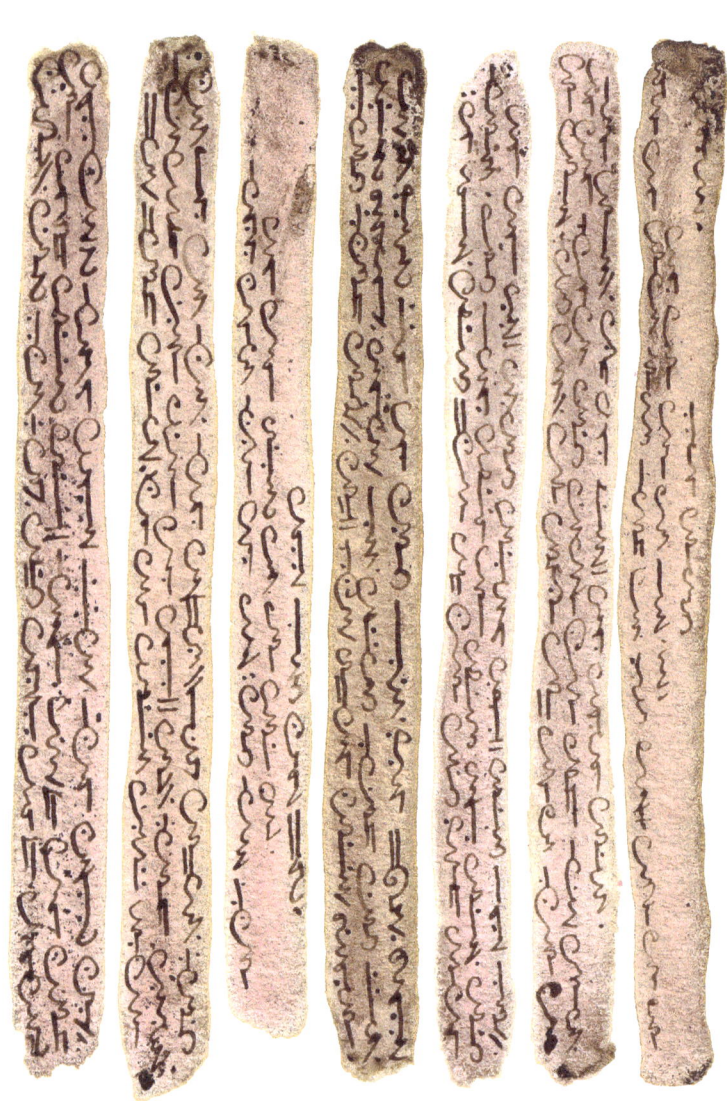

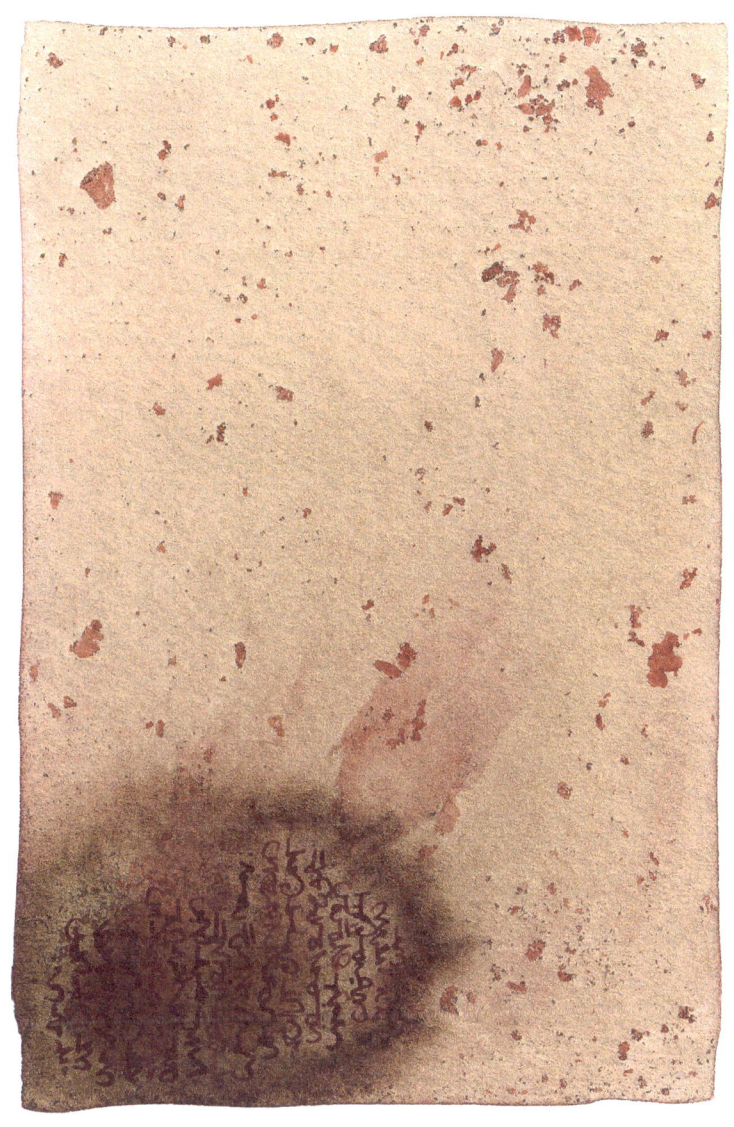

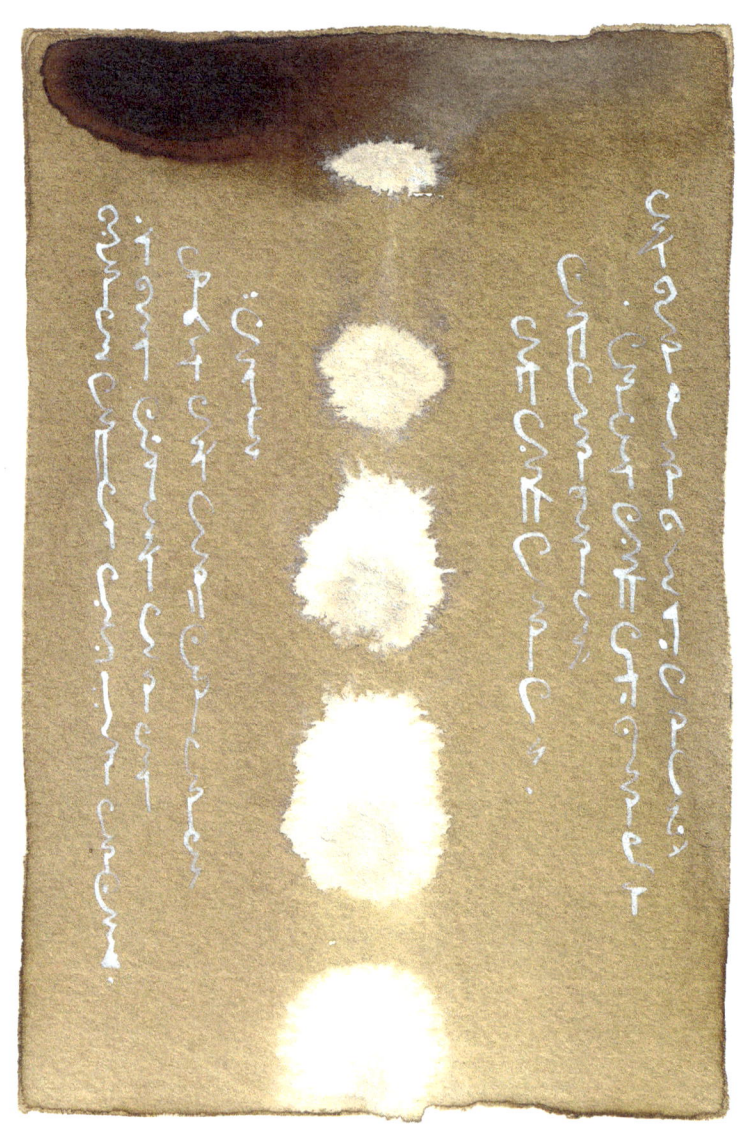

I listen into this empty and full space and then I place my pen or brush to the page and let my hand move. This is the practice of communicating with what is within me. With asemic writing I do not need to know anything more than this. No word required. No sense of meaning required. Just the willingness and desire to be in the process of making marks.

I look back at what I've written and although I know the truth in it, it is not the whole story. The river is that place in me, that sense of peaceful meditative attunement. It sounds good. A kind of perfection of nature and spiritual sensitivity. And that is genuine. The agitation that wells up in me is most often settled by a visit to the oxbow. All that true but not the full story. Good, happy, at peace is not always the true place of our feeling or even the necessary place to dwell and experience in our feeling selves. We are full of so many feeling states which are true and important, informative to the essence of our experience. Anger, grief, joy, passion, are just a few of them. And rarely are they pure states of feeling, anger is marbled with grief, joy with passion, passion with grief, you get my drift.

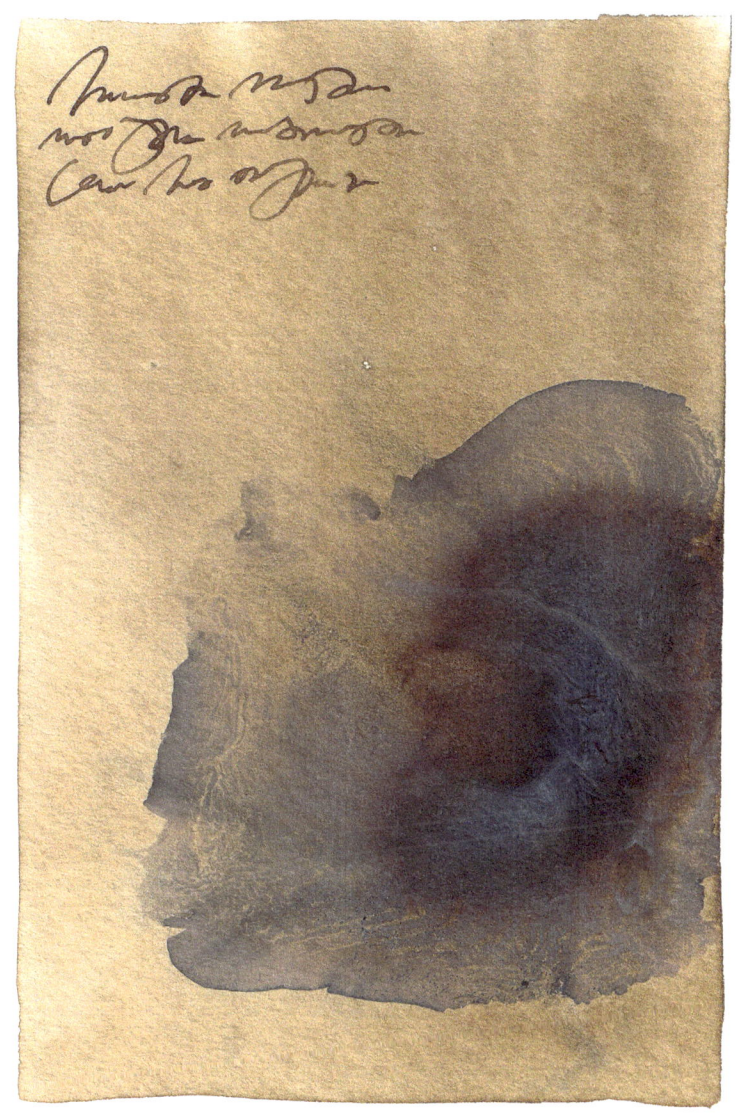

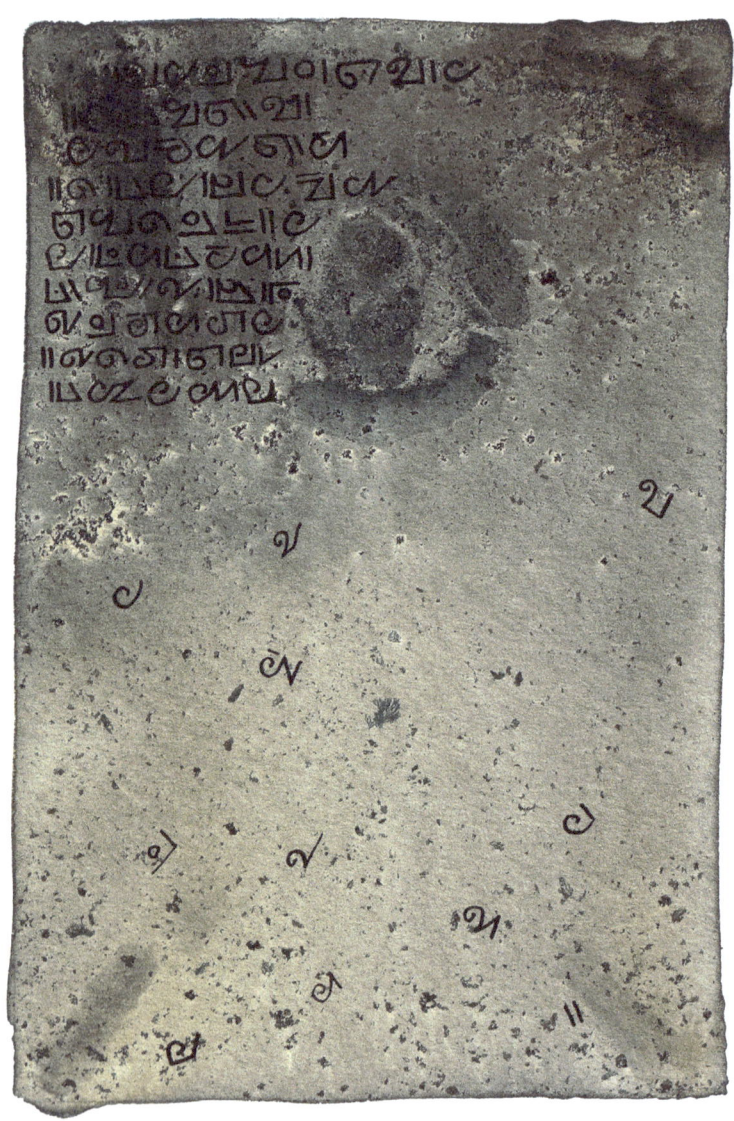

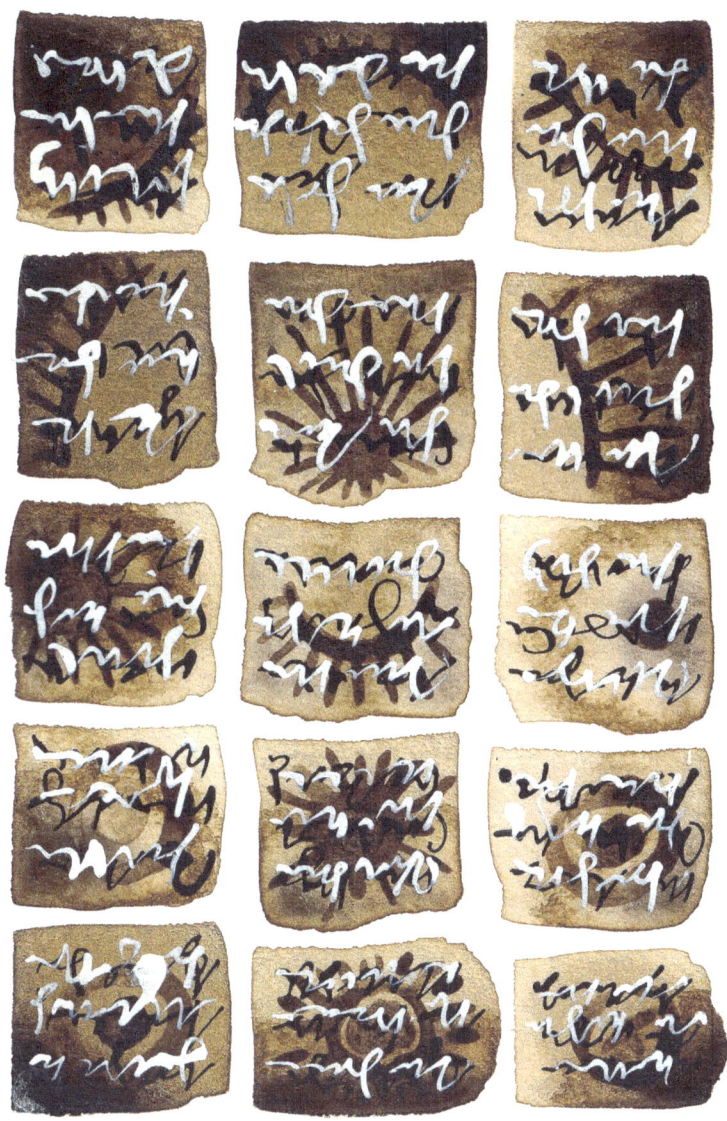

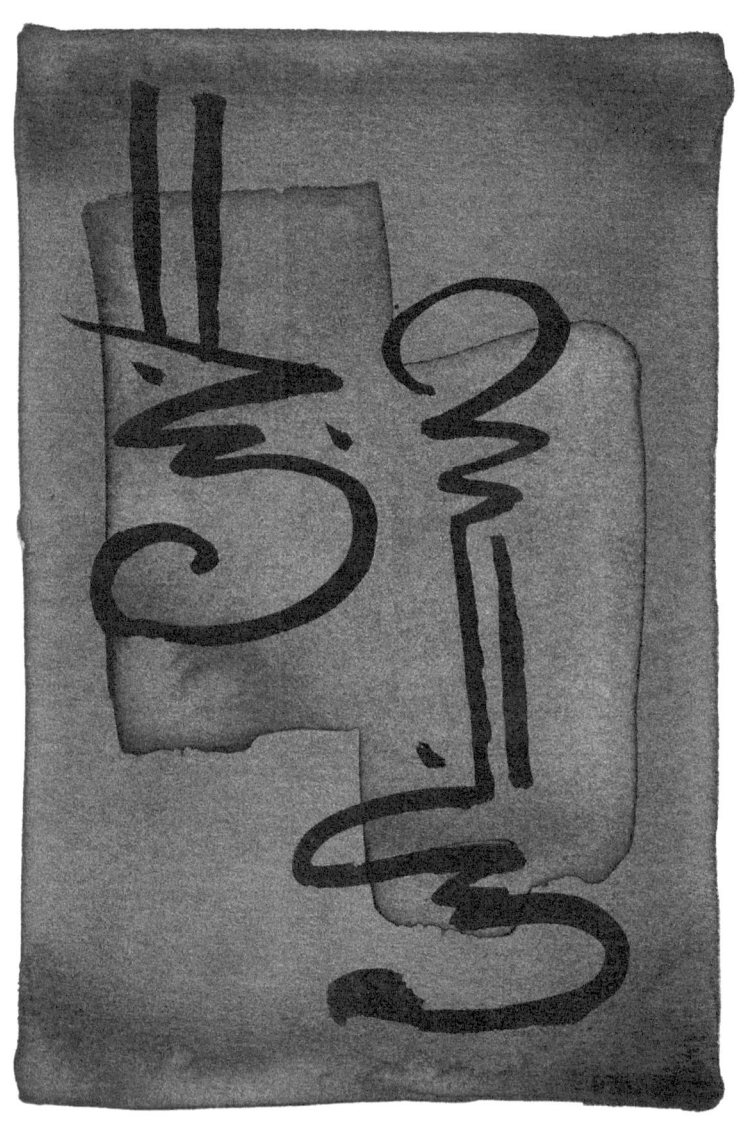

Still these states of experiential sensation, as uncomfortable as they can be, are worthy, just as worthy as peacefulness, contentedness. Kali, goddess of destruction in the Hindu faith, is associated with liberation and creation, and the Phoenix of Greek mythology must burn to ash to regenerate and be born again. These places also arise wordless and in need of gesture.

Let the hand move. Let my hand move. Let it move in the burning sensation of fire, of desolation, of crippling loneliness, in the bird flight or song of joy, in the mountain stream water or the consistent crash of ocean waves.

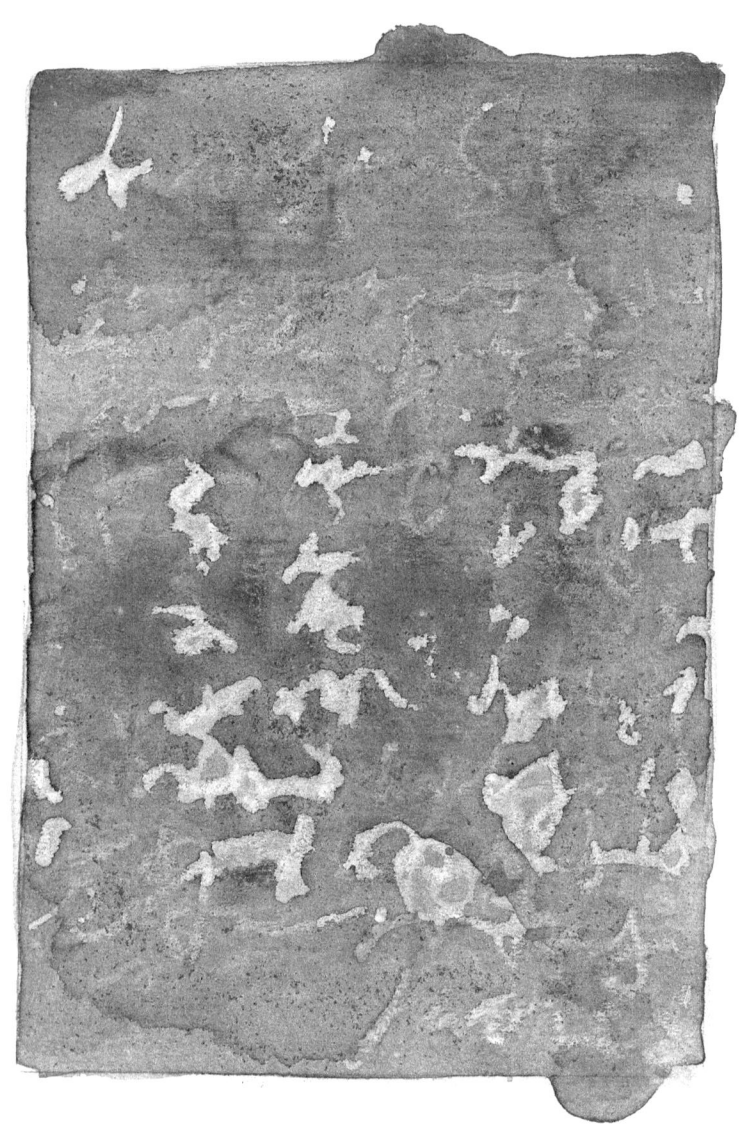

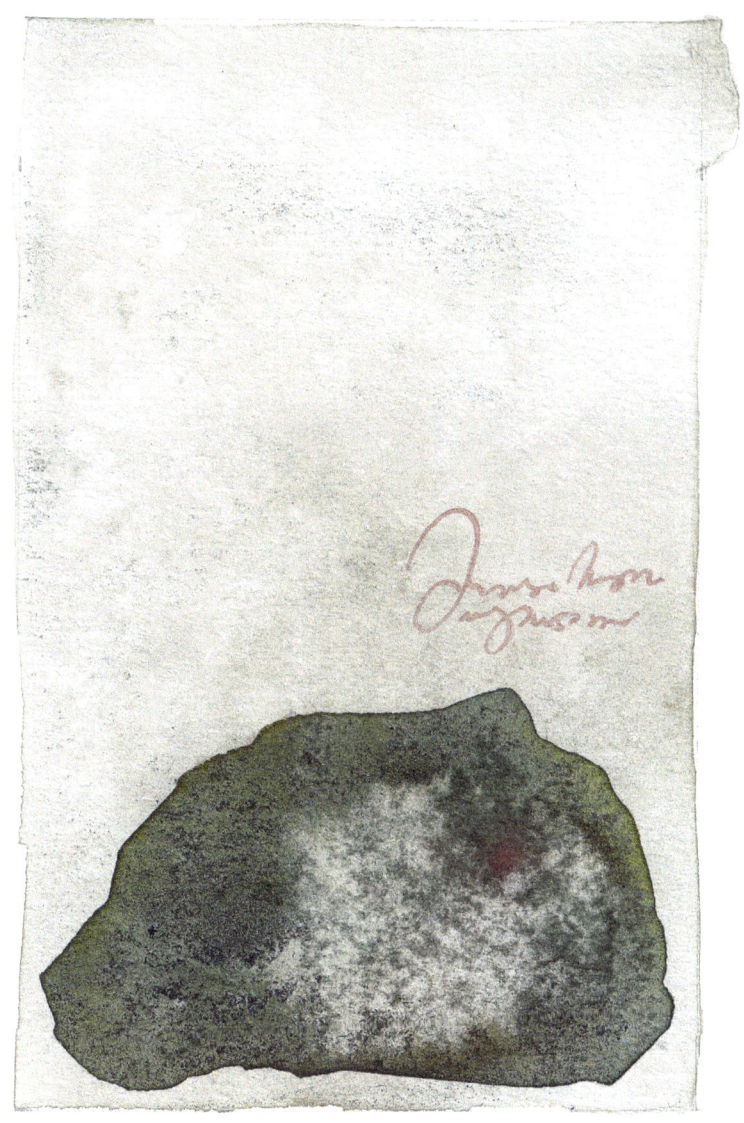

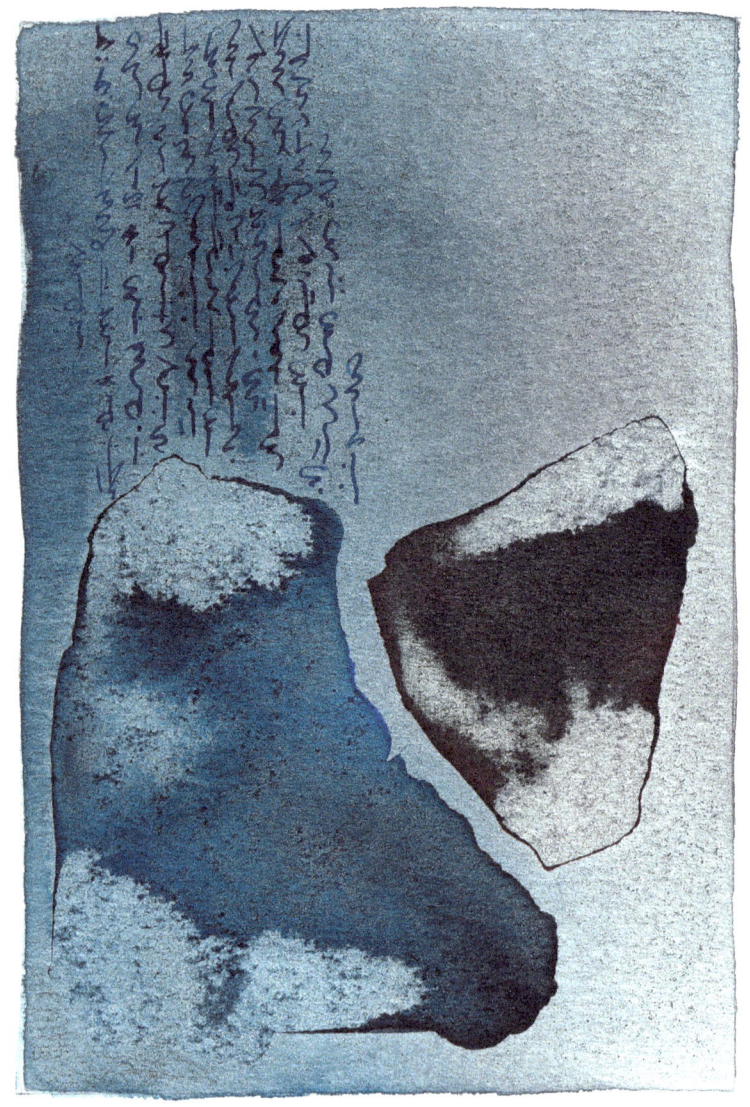

Looking back through my artwork I see I engaged with asemic writing for years before I understood what it was. But recently I turn to asemic writing deliberately as a way to not be silenced in the current political atmosphere where day after day horrific things are done in my name; it's unbearable. What can be said? It feels like too much but I refuse to be silenced, it is a radical act to not be silenced. And in this moment, it's the best I can do. I move my hand in radical gesture.

By making marks, I return to my body from the place of disassociation brought on by the news of children being ripped from the arms of their parents, the earth plundered for, well, everything, the cruelty of pitting us against each other and the cruelty which comes in the pitting. This news that can trigger my own personal trauma, is eased in gesture, in that return to my body. I am not necessarily made comfortable but what I feel is real. And there is a comfort in realness, in being aware and true to what is my experience in this world.

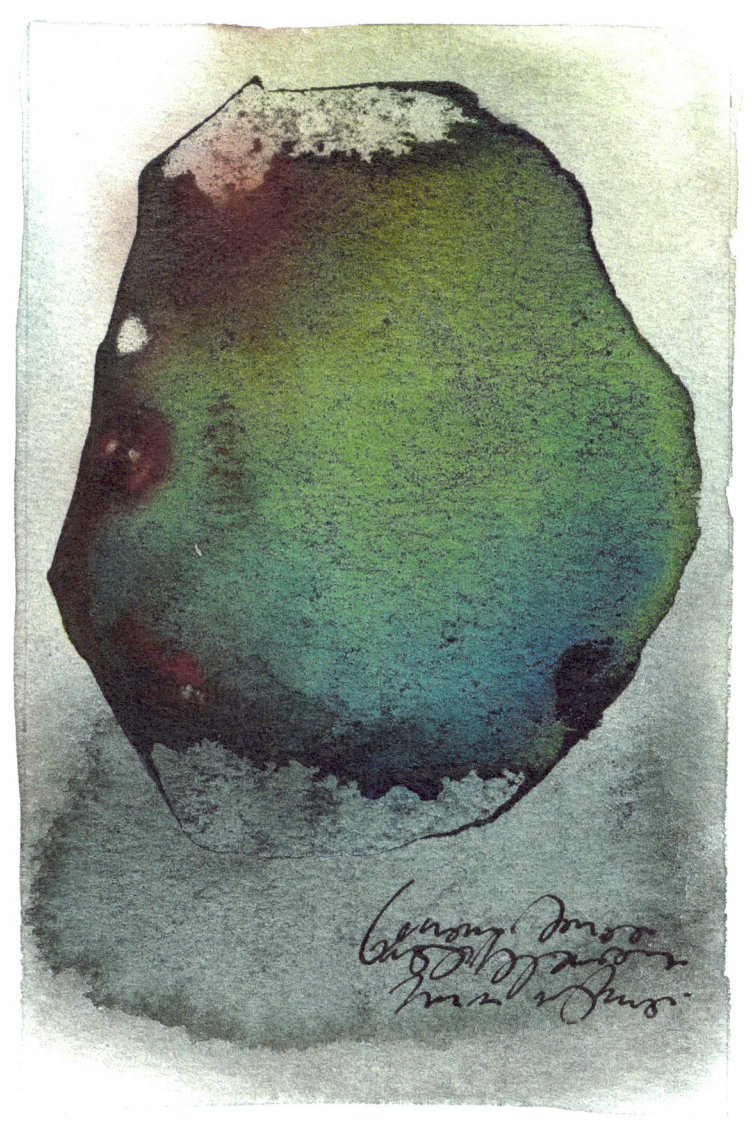

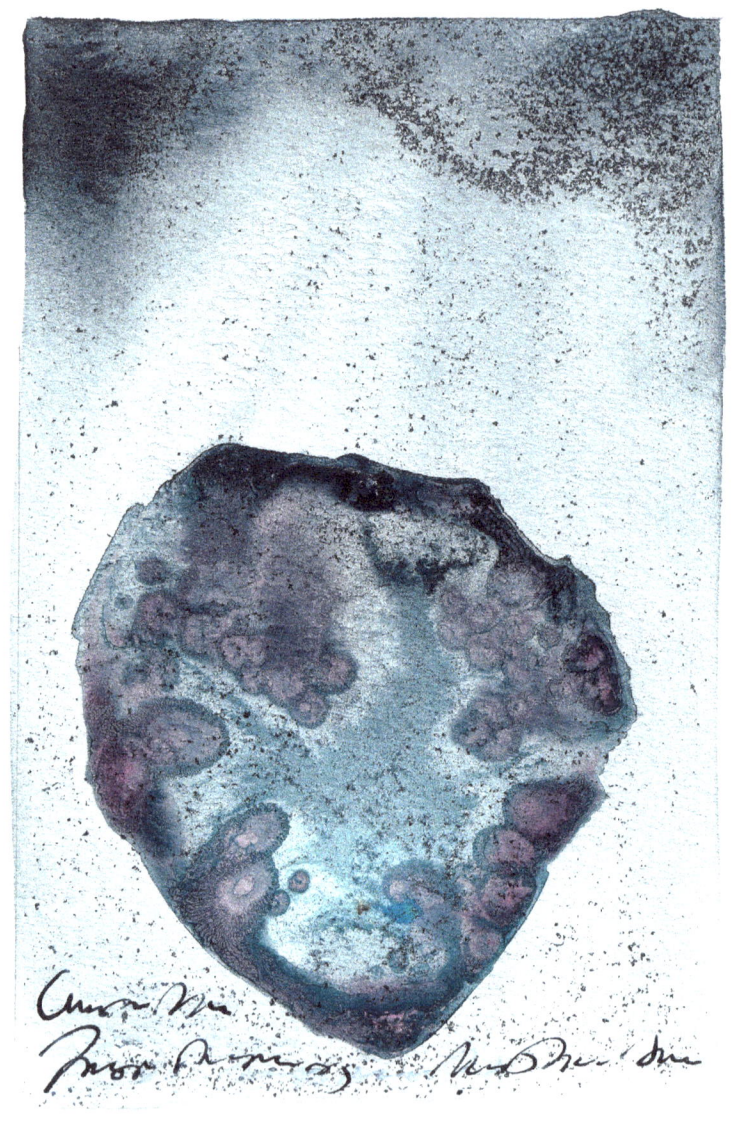

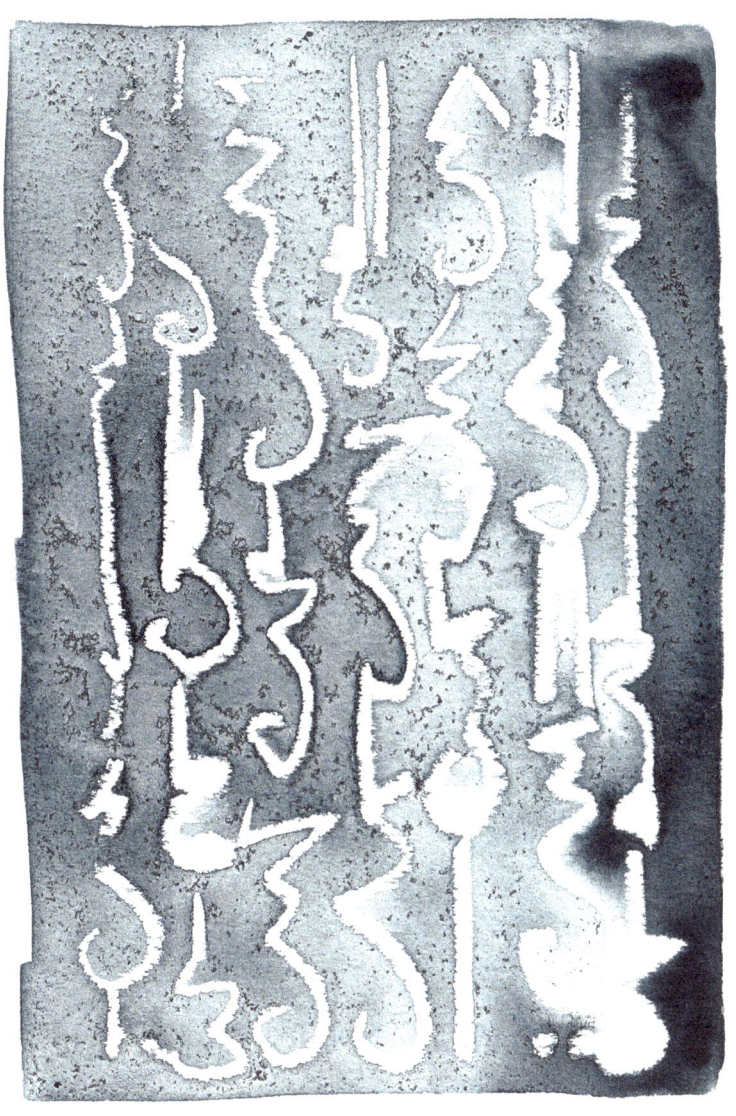

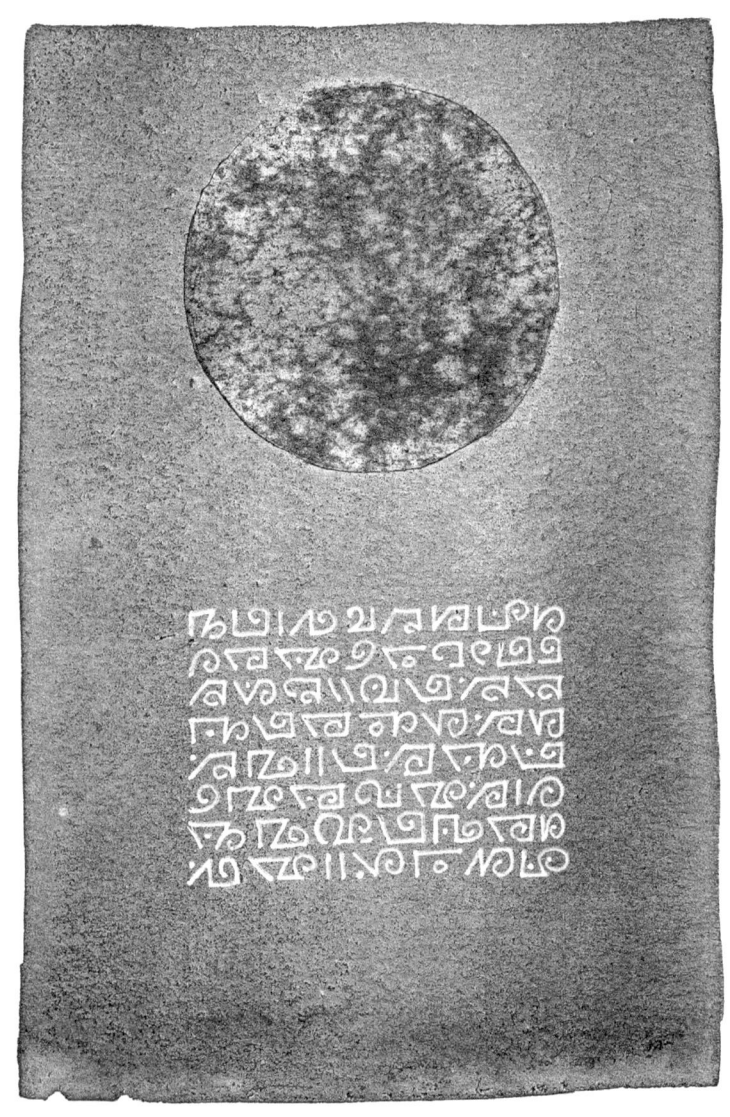

I dream the image of asemic writing over a moon, a variety of depictions of this image over and over again. This is the whole dream. I know I should paint this image to engage in it and to see what it will bring. I make a quick sketch of the image when I wake. I am after all someone who pays attention to my dreams, and I write my dream down whenever I wake with one. It takes me weeks to overcome my resistance to painting the image. I chose to make a large painting to match the dream, and when I finally have a canvas prepared I stand before it.

This big canvas, a white field, is like the snow covered vistas that are the landscape of Vermont in winter. In its negative, it is the cloud-covered night sky—dark and wide and empty. What mark will illuminate? I stand before the unknown, the empty blank bare plane of possibilities. This place can be overwhelming, anything could happen here. And then the first mark, the first field of color covers the canvas. I find my way. I begin to feel the power of the image and of my body expressing the image. I stand facing into a kind of fear, the fear of standing in the light of expressing what is coming through me, such a large painting, large expression, to bring into the world. It's uncomfortable. I recognize this feeling. When I start on a new piece that's calling to be painted, I often feel the power as resistance. I know I'm onto something good when this happens. And I often hate the piece, have to reason within myself as to why I'm following the call to paint it. Having engaged in this moment many times, I recognize the pattern and don't let it stop me.

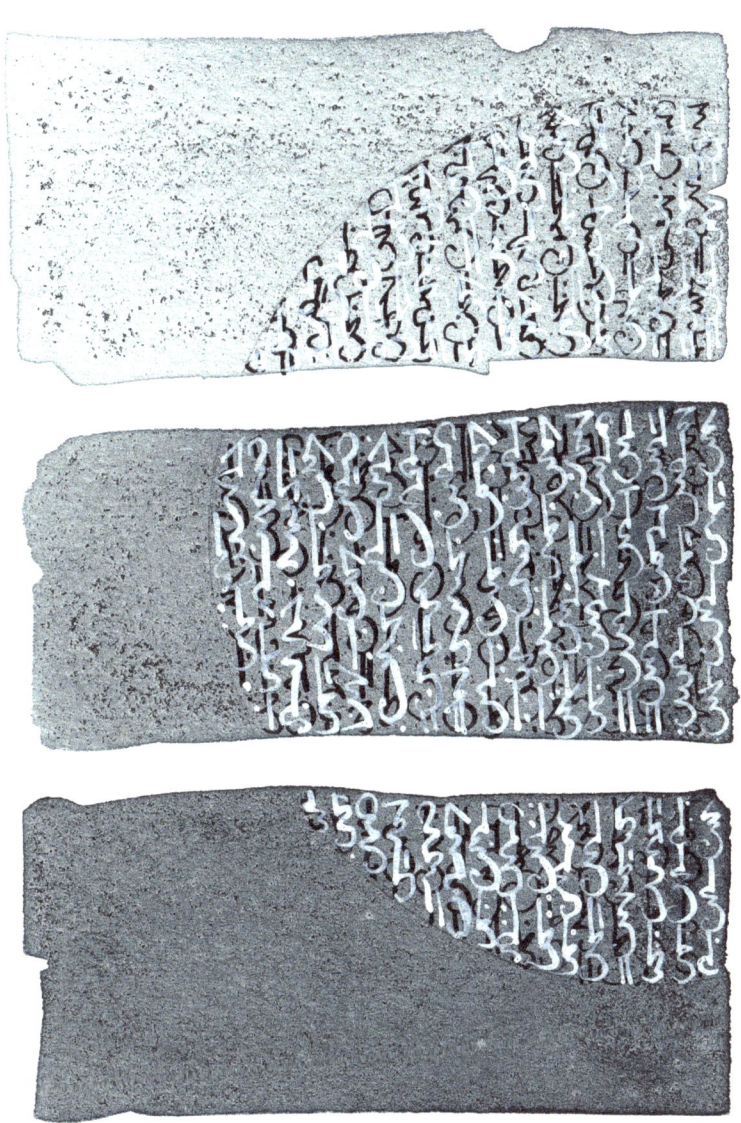

49

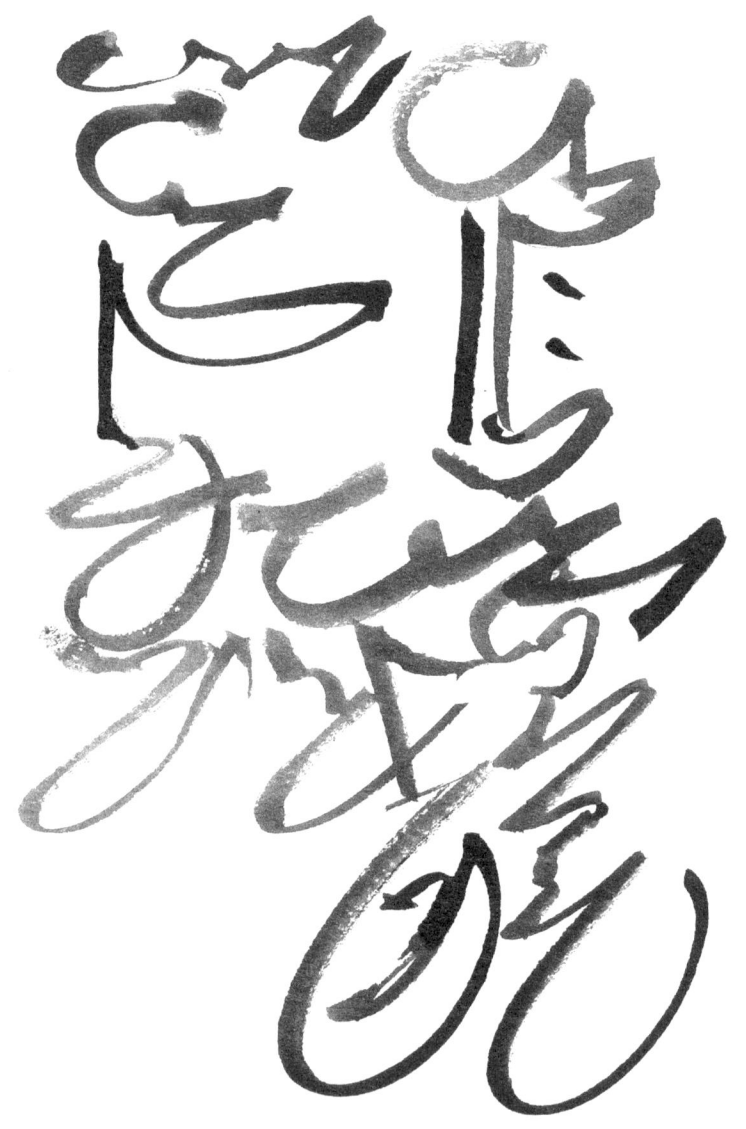

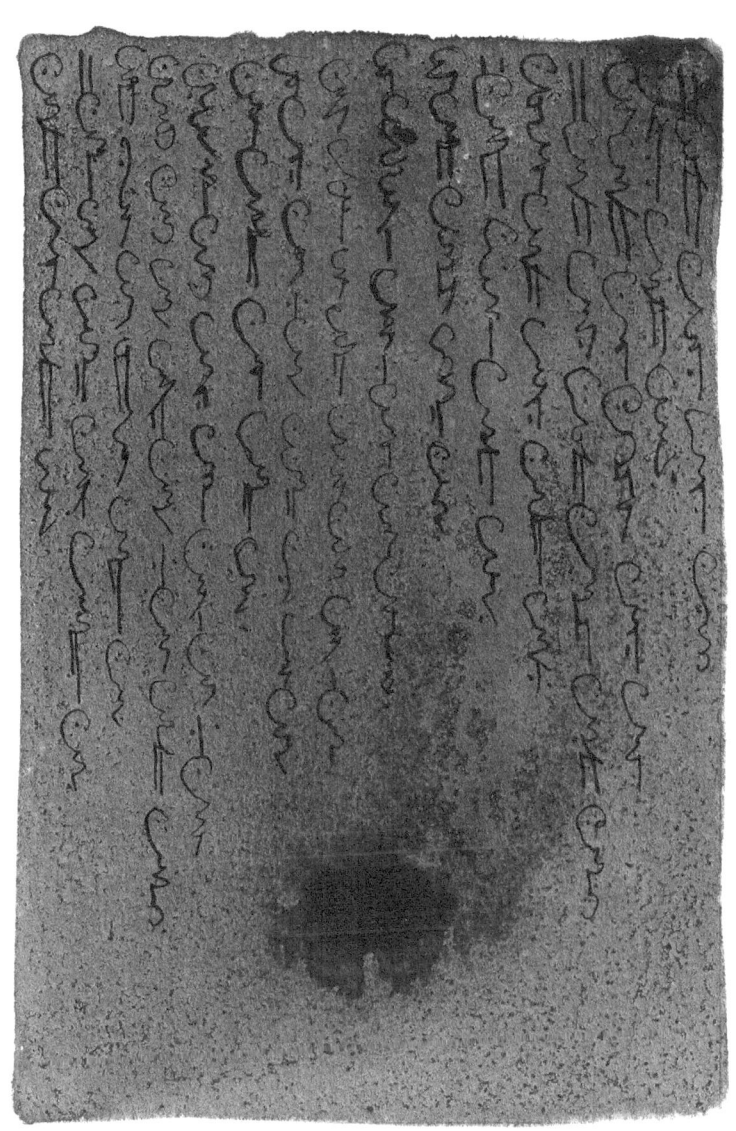

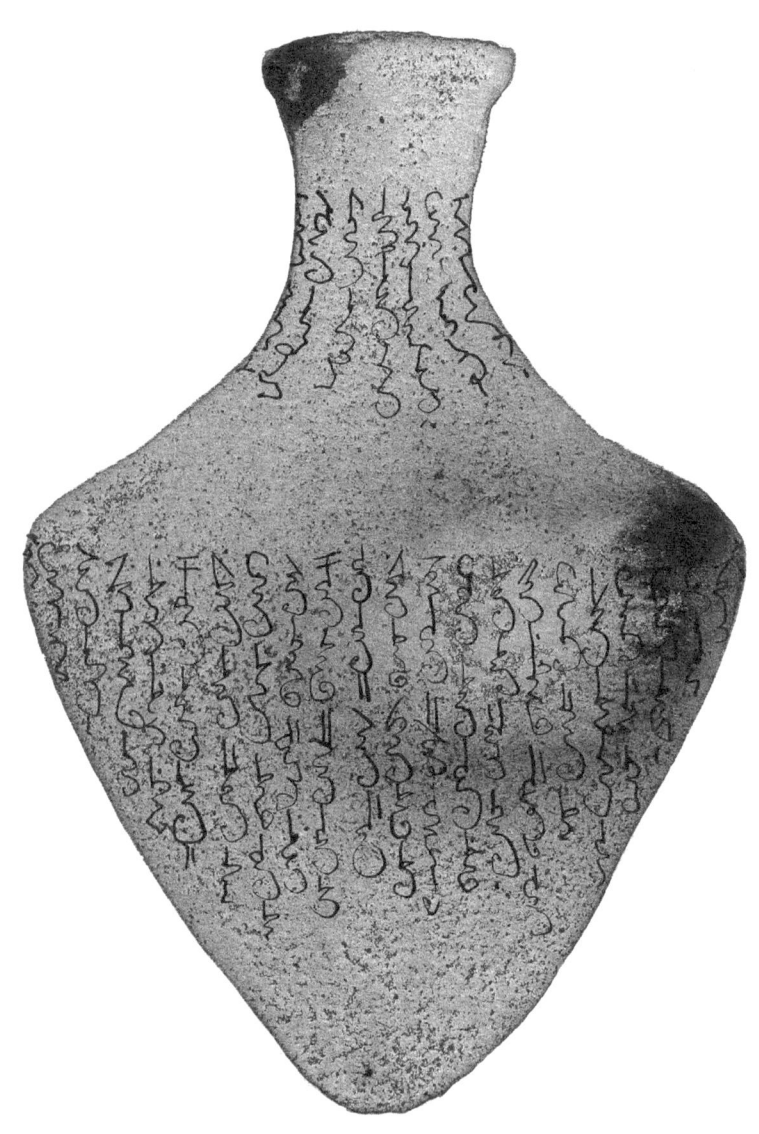

Why the moon I ask myself? Michael Meade speaks of this old idea of lunar knowledge, relates it to embodied knowledge, knowing things by heart. Meade says "as poets used to say, ideas live in the blood." This is a different source of knowing, not that which comes in the constant presence of the sun's light but in the ever changing light of the moon, the moon's light like the knowing of the body, always in flux, feelings moving through us. The moon, like the dream, showing us light in the darkness. I follow this light.

I can't tell you more about what or why it is important to start making these paintings, the large moon painting or these smaller day-pages, but I can feel within me some shift toward standing with myself. Do I need to know more than that? I want to tell you it's about this or that, but I don't yet know and may never know beyond what I've already said. I follow. It may be that to follow is the very meaning. And I am okay with that.

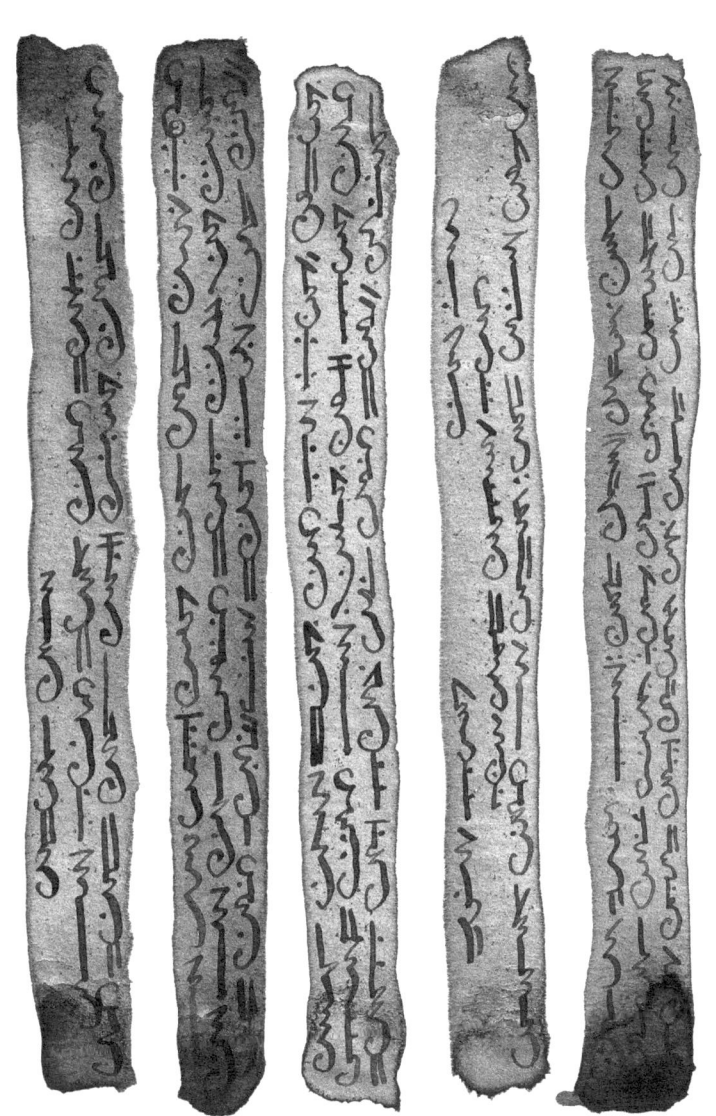

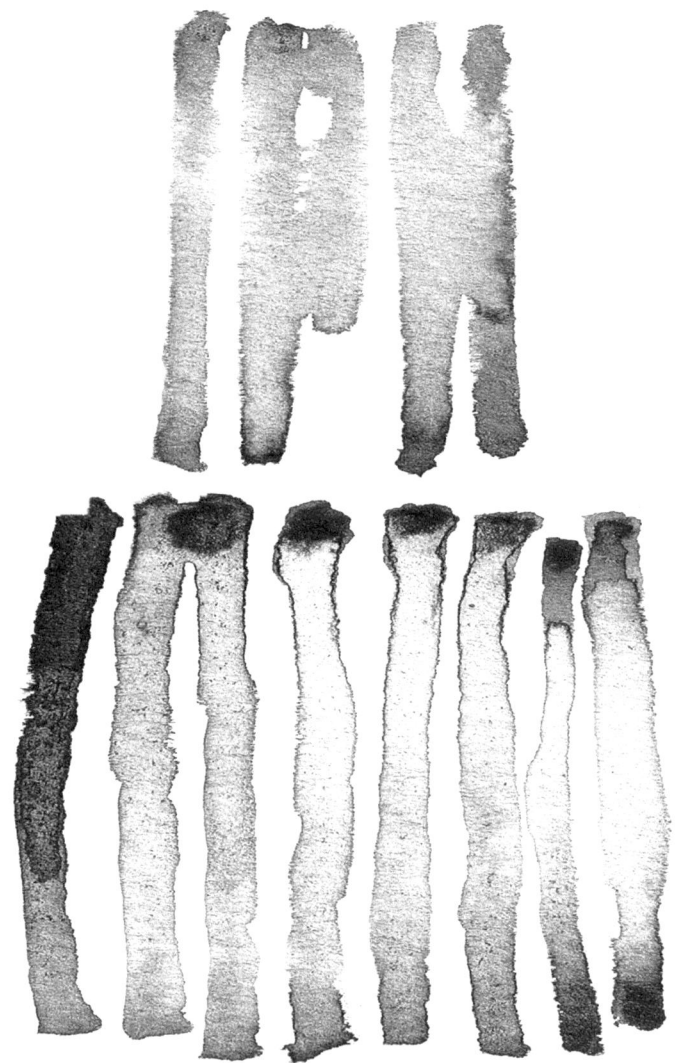

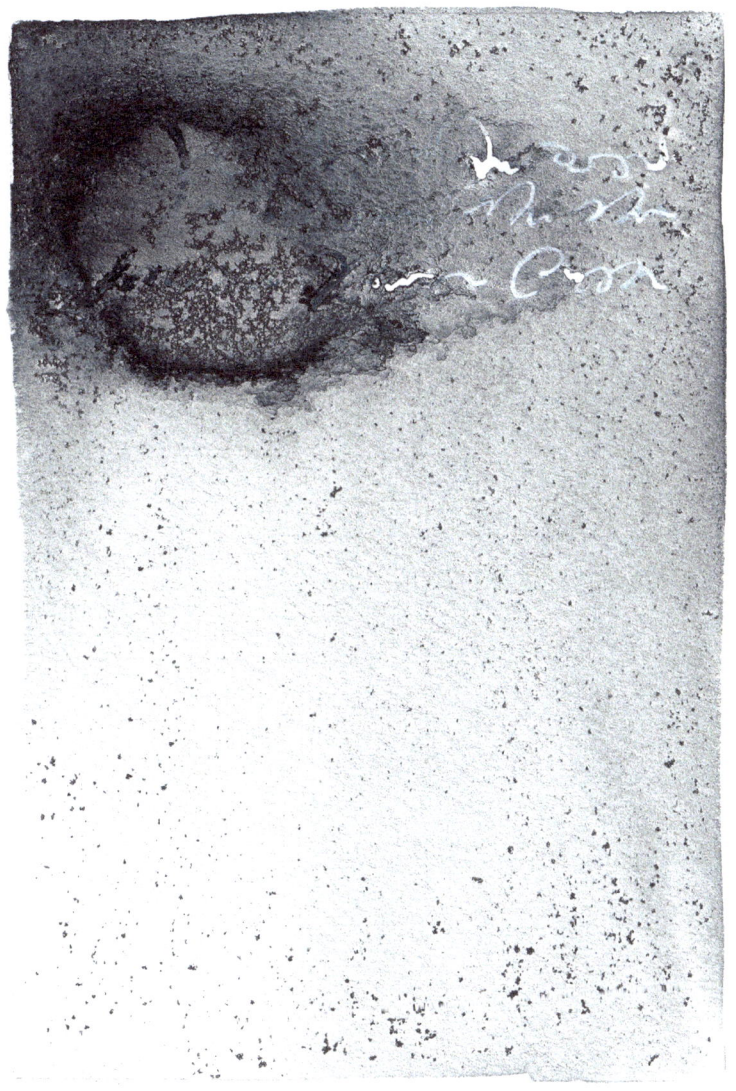

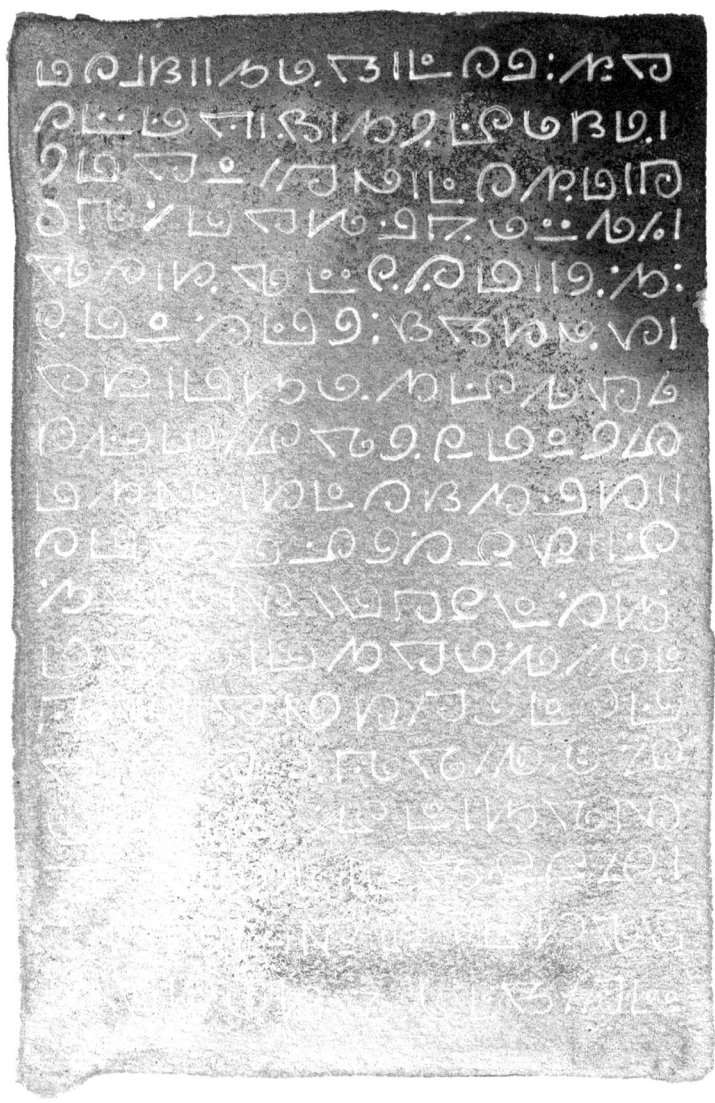

I turn to painting these smaller pieces on paper. I experiment with creating color fields with inks. I discover that the homemade inks I've made from black walnuts and hibiscus tea set in rubbing alcohol react to the store-bought inks and make curious patterns on the wetted paper. I write into these color fields. I am reminded of deteriorated book pages, and the asemic writing feels to me like ancient script. I am intrigued with what might be held in these gestures, in the markings I cannot with my logical mind read. If this is a book of spells or some coded knowledge or power, does just being a viewer transfigure their power?

As a reader or witness to the writing, do I need to know through the understanding of my mind? The spell works by giving me a feeling. That my feeling may be different than yours is not of importance. These works engage the viewer in a unique way, beyond more traditional abstract work, because the marks seem like one should be able to read them and that they are meant to be read. This awakens the part of the mind that engages with language, and in lieu of being given words with known meaning, the viewer creates their own translation, or meaning of what is written, entering, in a sense, a conversation with the piece, their own relationship with the piece.

The grass weaves its message to the viewer, person or deer, bird or worm. The sand holds its text, and I read what I read, you read what you read, feel what I feel, feel what you feel. In the branching tree limbs, in the waves, in my hand's scratching across paper, we each read the feeling that rises in us. Code, mark, emerging word, the experience of our being translates us into some form of knowing. *Is that not the power of this asemic work?*

Acknowledgments

I thank all who have been supportive of my work, and there are so many of you I cannot name you all. Know I am grateful for your encouragement and support. Thanks to all I have been inspired by—your words, your images, your actions. Personal thanks to Sue Scavo, who has stood by me as friend, as sister, as deepest supporter of who I am on all levels. Thanks to Jari Chealier who introduced me to *Asemic Writing: The New Post-Literate*, recognizing the work I had intuitively turned towards as asemic. In doing so, she sanctioned my work in the world. She introduced me to a community of people who hold the space of both poetry and art, people who understand the work's possibilities and with whom I can share what I do. I thank her also for sorting through paintings with me, helping me create a collection of images that are cohesive and hold the vision I intended. Thanks to Kristine Snodgrass who reached out to me from that community in support and love of my work, as well as creating a further space to share in Women Asemic Artists & Visual Poets // WAAVe Global. Thanks to David Mattingly who also reached out from the asemic community, who dived deeply into the theoretics of asemics with me, via correspondence, helping me refine my own ideas and feelings around asemic writing, and who graciously read my essay and responded with support and encouragement. I also thank Peter Lourie who spent a great deal of time encouraging me to write about my art process and who read drafts of this essay time and time again; I wouldn't have written it without his incredible support of me, my writing, and my path forward on this journey. Thanks to Elizabeth Powell, an ardent supporter; her enthusiasm for my work has been a cornerstone to me. And thanks to Martine Bisagni who took the time and used her expertise to take photos of my work so they would best represent my paintings. Thanks to my sweet sweet daughter, Sadie Newman, who knows me so well and has taught me much about love, spirit, and fearlessly entering the world. And to all my family who support and love me. I thank the dream that inserted itself into my consciousness and allowed me to follow that dream and all the dreams that have led me towards a full life. And lastly, Christine Cote, for being a devoted supporter of my work, publishing my first two books of poems with Shanti Arts, publishing my work in *Still Point Arts Quarterly*, and for taking a chance on asemic writing by publishing *Fluency*. She has been an incredible source of confidence in my self and my journey in this world.

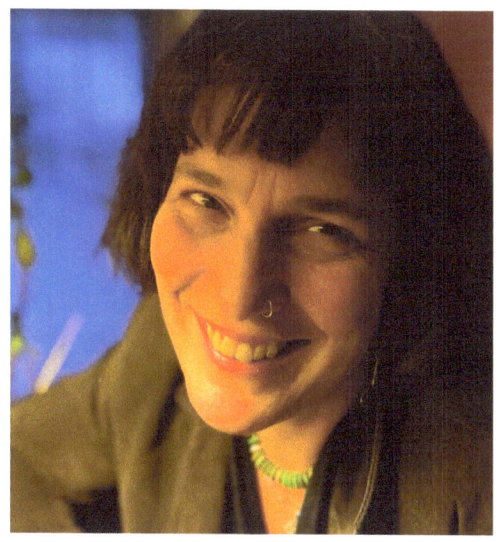

KARLA VAN VLIET is the author of *From the Book of Remembrance* and *The River from My Mouth*, collections of poetry and paintings, both published by Shanti Arts; and a poem-length chapbook, *Fragments: From the Lost Book of the Bird Spirit*, published by Folded Word. Van Vliet's book *She Speaks in Tongues*, a collection of poems and asemic writings, is forthcoming from Anhinga Press. She is an Edna St. Vincent Millay Poetry Prize finalist, and a two-time Pushcart and Best of the Net nominee. Her poems have appeared in *Acumen, Poet Lore, The Tishman Review, Green Mountains Review, Crannog Magazine*, and others.

Karla's paintings have been featured in *Women Asemic Writers, UTSANGA.IT, Still Point Art Quarterly, Stone Voices Magazine, Champlain's Lake Rediscovered,* and *Gate Posts with No Gate: The Leg Paint Project.* She is a member of WAAVe Global (Women Asemic Artists & Visual Poets) and Asemic Writing: The New Post-Literate.

Karla is a co-founder and editor of *deLuge Journal*. She is an Integrative Dreamwork analyst, artist, and administrator of the New England Young Writers' Conference at Bread Loaf, Middlebury College. Karla lives in Vermont, USA.

For purchase of original art visit:

www.vanvlietarts.com

www.vanvlietgallery.com

www.ingramcontent.com/pod-product-compliance
Lightning Source LLC
Chambersburg PA
CBHW040323220526
45473CB00009B/2548